D1404212

VICTORS VALIANT

GO BLUE

THE MOST SPECTACULAR SIGHTS
& SOUNDS OF MICHIGAN FOOTBALL

VICTORS VALIANT

THE MOST SPECTACULAR SIGHTS & SOUNDS OF MICHIGAN FOOTBALL

ATHLON® SPORTS™

RUTLEDGE HILL PRESS™
NASHVILLE, TENNESSEE

A DIVISION OF THOMAS NELSON PUBLISHERS, INC.
WWW.THOMASNELSON.COM

COPYRIGHT © 2003 BY ATHLON® SPORTS™

All rights reserved. No portion of this book may be reproduced, stored in a retrieval system, or transmitted in any form or by any means—electronic, mechanical, photocopy, recording, or any other—except for brief quotations in printed reviews, without the prior permission of the publisher.

Published by Rutledge Hill Press, a Division of Thomas Nelson, Inc., P.O. Box 141000, Nashville, Tennessee, 37214.

1-4016-0102-2

Printed in the United States of America
03 04 05 06 07—5 4 3 2 1

TABLE of CONTENTS

ACKNOWLEDGMENTS   VI

INTRODUCTION   VII

TRADITIONS AND PAGEANTRY   1

GREAT COACHES   19

GREAT RIVALRIES   24

GREAT TEAMS   32

GREAT PLAYERS   38

MICHIGAN IN THE COLLEGE FOOTBALL HALL OF FAME   47

TALKING MICHIGAN FOOTBALL   49

BOWL GAME TRADITION   52

ACKNOWLEDGMENTS

Athlon Sports would like to thank Rutledge Hill Press, Kevin Daniels, Tony Hagelgans, Greg Karmizan, the College Football Hall of Fame, the University of Michigan Sports Information office, the Bob Ufer family, and above all the Michigan fans, whose passionate devotion to their Wolverines defines what college football is all about.

INTRODUCTION

In its 123 years of intercollegiate competition, the University of Michigan has won more football games (823) than any other program in Division I-A. No other school has won more conference titles than Michigan's 40 in the Big Ten, and Michigan's 11 national titles tie the school for fourth all-time. The Wolverines have appeared in bowl games for 28 consecutive years.

All this to say — when it comes to college football, nobody's done it better or for longer than the University of Michigan. From Fielding Yost's Point-a-Minute teams, to Bennie Oosterbaan and the 1948 champs, to Bo Schembechler's storied run as coach of the Wolverines, to the Heisman campaigns of Tom Harmon, Desmond Howard and Charles Woodson, to the 1997 National Championship, the Michigan program is more than an important part of college football history. It *is* college football history.

...WHEN IT COMES TO COLLEGE FOOTBALL, NOBODY'S DONE IT BETTER OR FOR LONGER THAN THE UNIVERSITY OF MICHIGAN.

On the pages that follow, we present a snapshot of the traditions, the memories, the indelible images that make up the tapestry of Michigan football. So, as the storied fight song puts it so eloquently, Hail! to the Victors Valiant.

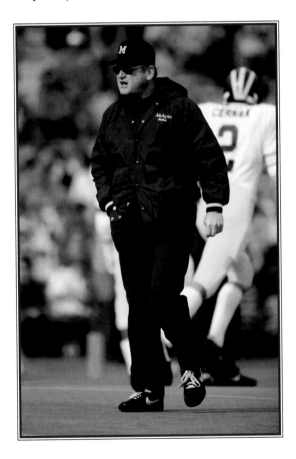

TRADITIONS AND PAGEANTRY

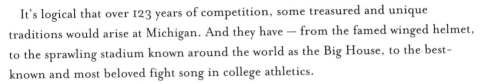

It's logical that over 123 years of competition, some treasured and unique traditions would arise at Michigan. And they have — from the famed winged helmet, to the sprawling stadium known around the world as the Big House, to the best-known and most beloved fight song in college athletics.

Taken collectively, these are more than traditions. They're the very fabric of a university, the pride of a worldwide community of those who bleed maize and blue.

WOLVERINES

How Michigan acquired the nickname "Wolverines" is shrouded in mystery. As far as anyone knows, the ferocious carnivore is not indigenous to the state, but Michiganders have carried the moniker at least since the border dispute with Ohio known as the "Toledo War" in 1803. Researchers have speculated that its origin dates back to the days of the fur trade, when Sault Ste. Marie served as a hub for wolverine pelts in the 1700s. In 1927, a pair of wolverines named Bennie and Biff were paraded around Michigan Stadium in cages on game days. However, their nasty dispositions led to their retirement after just one season.

MAIZE AND BLUE

Azure blue and maize were adopted as the official colors of the University of Michigan on February 12, 1867, by a student committee from the Literary Department. Later, around the turn of the twentieth century, the school's athletic teams decided on deep blue and bright yellow for their uniform colors.

HAIL TO THE VICTORS

A 12–11 Michigan win over national powerhouse Chicago in the 1898 season finale brought the Wolverines' final ledger to 10–0 and secured the Western Intercollegiate Conference (later known as the Big Ten) championship. While celebrating the victory, Louis Elbel noted with some dismay the lack of a proper celebration song. The Michigan Band played "Hot Time in the Old Town," and Elbel, a U-M music student, felt it didn't measure up to the moment. He composed "The Victors" on the train back to Ann Arbor from Chicago. The now-famous march was performed for the first time in 1899 by none other than John Philip Sousa, while his band was making an appearance in Ann Arbor.

LYRICS TO "THE VICTORS"

Now for a cheer they are here, triumphant!

Here they come with banners flying.

In stalwart step they're nighing.

With shouts of vict'ry crying.

We hurrah, hurrah, we greet you now, Hail!

Far we their praises sing

For the glory and fame they've bro't us,

Loud let the bells them ring,

For here they come with banners flying

Far we their praises tell

For the glory and fame they've bro't us,

Loud let the bells them ring

For here they come with banners flying

Here they come, Hurrah!

Hail! To the victors valiant

Hail! To the conqu'ring heroes

Hail! Hail! To Michigan

The leaders and the best

Hail! To the victors valiant

Hail! To the conqu'ring heroes

Hail! Hail! To Michigan

The champions of the West!

GO BLUE

THE WINGED HELMET

One of the most distinctive symbols in all of college football is the winged helmet worn by Michigan football players. Before Fritz Crisler arrived as head coach from Princeton in 1938, the football team wore plain black helmets. Crisler added the winged design "to dress it up a little," he claimed. He also felt the unique design would aid his quarterbacks in spotting their receivers downfield. The results? Compared to their 1937 numbers, the 1938 Wolverines' completion percentage and touchdown passes skyrocketed while cutting interceptions almost in half. Though the maize wings and stripes were simply painted over design elements of the early leather headgear, the decorative color code was retained to honor the school's great winning tradition as the helmet has evolved in material and shape.

THE MICHIGAN MARCHING BAND

The organization known today as the Michigan Marching Band began in 1844 as a nine-man contingent. Since then it has grown to a 225-piece band that performs at all Michigan home games and bowl appearances, as it has now for 103 years. In 1950, the Michigan Marching Band was dubbed the "Transcontinental Band" after playing at both Yankee Stadium and the Rose Bowl that season. It was the Michigan Band that originated the "Script Ohio," which it introduced to the world on October 15, 1932, in Columbus, Ohio, to honor its Ohio State hosts that day. The inaugural Sudler Trophy, awarded annually to the nation's top college marching band, was bestowed upon the Michigan Marching Band in 1983.

GAME DAY

The Michigan Marching Band leads the way from campus to the stadium entrance before each home game, with a thousand or more fans in its wake. The golf course across from the stadium is premium tailgating real estate. Fans navigate more than a hundred rows of seats in Michigan Stadium, the nation's largest football stadium, to take their places and await the arrival of their team. As game time approaches, the players burst from the tunnel and run onto the field under the Michigan Football banner. Players and cheerleaders alike jump up to touch it as they stream underneath.

MICHIGAN STADIUM

On September 4, 1999, Michigan established a new NCAA single-game attendance record as 111,523 fans witnessed the Wolverines defeat Notre Dame 26–22. The figure eclipsed the old record set by — you guessed it — Michigan, on September 26, 1998. Michigan has led the nation in average home-game attendance for 28 of the last 29 years. The average crowd of 110,576 in Michigan Stadium in 2002 outpaced second-place Penn State by well over 3,000 fans per game.

Michigan Stadium was dedicated on October 22, 1927, with a 21–0 victory over Ohio State. The facility was filled to capacity with 84,401 in attendance for the event. There have been periodic expansion projects over the years leading to the current seating capacity of 107,501, making Michigan Stadium, a.k.a. "The Big House," the largest football stadium in the country.

"THE BIG HOUSE," THE LARGEST FOOTBALL STADIUM IN THE COUNTRY.

BOB UFER

Michigan football fans will always remember Bob Ufer, the Voice of "Meechigan" football. His five-decade broadcasting career spanned 363 consecutive games from 1945 to 1981. A University of Michigan athlete in his own right, Bob played freshman football with the legendary Tom Harmon and went on to set U of M track records in all events from the 100- to the 800-yard dash. He held a world record in the 440-yard dash for three years.

Bob's love of Michigan led him into the broadcast booth, where his "Uferisms" became legendary. Who will ever forget the George Patton scoring horn and Bob's accounts of "General George Bo Patton Schembechler" and "Dr. Strange Hayes"? Those who remember the Michigan football greats (Yost, Oosterbaan, Crisler, Schembechler and Harmon) agree that Bob belongs on that list. Ufer's passion for Michigan football was evident to all who heard him, proving that indeed "football is a religion and Saturday is the holy day of obligation." For more information on the Bob Ufer Scholarship Fund/Foundation, visit www.ufer.org or call 800-216-4166.

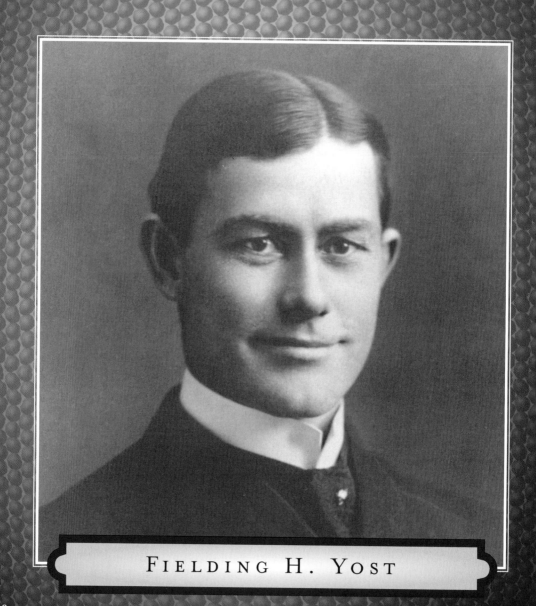

FIELDING H. YOST

GREAT COACHES

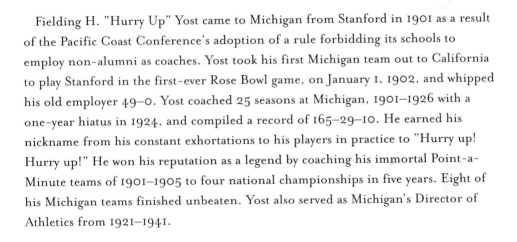

Fielding H. "Hurry Up" Yost came to Michigan from Stanford in 1901 as a result of the Pacific Coast Conference's adoption of a rule forbidding its schools to employ non-alumni as coaches. Yost took his first Michigan team out to California to play Stanford in the first-ever Rose Bowl game, on January 1, 1902, and whipped his old employer 49–0. Yost coached 25 seasons at Michigan, 1901–1926 with a one-year hiatus in 1924, and compiled a record of 165–29–10. He earned his nickname from his constant exhortations to his players in practice to "Hurry up! Hurry up!" He won his reputation as a legend by coaching his immortal Point-a-Minute teams of 1901–1905 to four national championships in five years. Eight of his Michigan teams finished unbeaten. Yost also served as Michigan's Director of Athletics from 1921–1941.

Fritz Crisler's winning percentage of .805 (71–16–3) over his 10 years from 1938–1947 ranks second in school history behind only Yost's .833. His 1947 team finished 10–0, won the national title and beat USC 49–0 in the Rose Bowl. Crisler played football at the University of Chicago under Amos Alonzo Stagg and stayed on at Chicago as a Stagg assistant for eight years. He held head coaching positions at Minnesota and Princeton before bringing his innovative approach — and the winged helmet — to Ann Arbor. At a time when most teams were switching to the T-formation, Crisler stuck faithfully to the single wing. His buck lateral and spinner-cycle offense, requiring flawless timing, ball-handling and execution, was a thrill to watch.

HERBERT O. "FRITZ" CRISLER

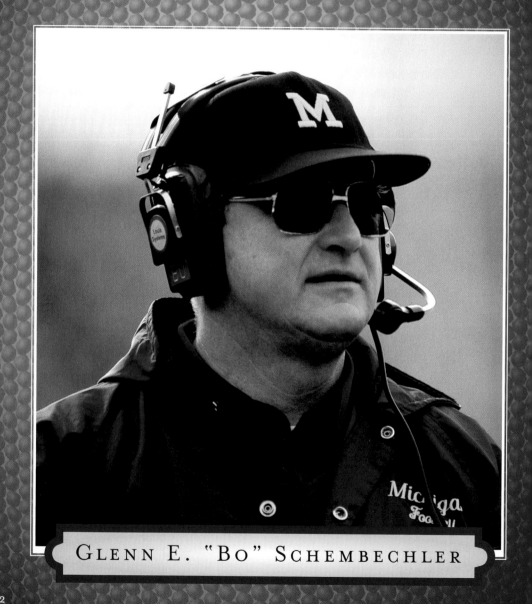

GLENN E. "BO" SCHEMBECHLER

GO BLUE

Bo Schembechler, one of the fiercest competitors ever to inhabit the coaching profession, won 80 percent of his games as Michigan's head man. In 21 years at the helm, from 1969–89, he amassed more wins than any other Michigan coach, compiling a record of 194–48–5. Schembechler, a product of the Miami (Ohio) coaching factory, guided the Wolverines to the nation's best regular-season record in the decade of the seventies at 96–10–3. He took 17 of his teams to postseason appearances, including 10 Rose Bowls. His teams won or shared 13 Big Ten titles, taking the last two of his career — in 1988 and 1989 — outright. When he retired in 1989, Schembechler was the fifth-winningest coach in Division I-A history, with 234 career victories.

GREAT RIVALRIES

OHIO STATE

Ohio State and Michigan have met 99 times, with Michigan holding a 56–37–6 advantage.

The first Michigan–Ohio State game, played on October 16, 1897, ended in a 34–0 Michigan triumph. The Wolverines easily handled the Buckeyes in that first encounter. In fact, Ohio State failed to score in its first five meetings with Michigan and eight of the first nine.

Fielding H. Yost's 1902 club waxed the Buckeyes 86–0. It was not until 1919, with Yost still at the controls in Ann Arbor, that Ohio State managed to beat the Wolverines — on its sixteenth try.

Since 1935, the Michigan–Ohio State game has been played on the final Saturday of the Big Ten season. Since then, 19 of the match-ups have been winner-take-all in the Big Ten race. Every year from 1972–1981, the winner of the game emerged with the Rose Bowl bid. Ohio Stadium's dedication game, in 1922, was against Michigan. Michigan Stadium's dedication game was in 1927 against Ohio State. The Wolverines blanked the Buckeyes both times.

You can drag up a lot of memories about this old rivalry, but the ones that seem to stand out above all the others are the "Snow Bowl" game and the personal battles between Woody Hayes and Bo Schembechler.

The Snow Bowl was played in 1950 at Columbus. The state of Ohio was buried under a foot of snow, and it blew so hard around Ohio Stadium it was almost impossible to see. The field was completely obliterated. Nobody had any idea where the yard lines were. There were several inches of snow on the ground, piles of snow stacked around the field and more coming down every minute. The temperature registered near zero and the wind was blowing through the stadium at 28 miles per hour, creating a minus-29-degree wind chill. The teams would run a play and then the sweepers would race on the field to see where the ball was resting. They sold 82,300 tickets for the game and, amazingly, 50,503 showed up in those miserable conditions. Michigan won 9–3 without making a first down, completing a pass or having a run of over six yards. The Wolverines' points came on a safety and a touch-down off a blocked punt. The win secured for coach Bennie Oosterbaan's Michigan team its fourth straight Big Ten title.

Bo Schembechler took over as Michigan's coach in 1969. That season, Bo pulled off the biggest upset in the history of the rivalry, whipping Hayes' top-ranked Buckeyes 24–12 and destroying OSU's otherwise perfect season. It was the start of a personal rivalry that would burn intensely until Hayes' departure following the 1978 season.

The Big Ten became known as the "Big Two and Little Eight" during the Hayes-

---

THAT SEASON, BO PULLED OFF THE BIGGEST UPSET IN THE HISTORY OF THE RIVALRY, WHIPPING HAYES' TOP-RANKED BUCKEYES 24 – 12 AND DESTROYING OSU'S OTHERWISE PERFECT SEASON.

Schembechler years. Michigan and Ohio State simply dominated the conference, winning or sharing every championship in the 10 seasons their teams met.

Lloyd Carr, one of the five winningest coaches in Division I-A, is the current custodian of Michigan's proud football program. Carr took over in 1995, won his first three meetings with the Buckeyes and currently stands at 5–3 in the rivalry.

NOTRE DAME

Here's a little-known item of football trivia: Michigan taught Notre Dame how to play football. The first three football games Notre Dame ever played were against Michigan — one in 1887 and two in 1888 — and Michigan won all three. In fact, the Wolverines prevailed in their first eight matchups with the Fighting Irish. The rivalry isn't renewed every year, but since Michigan and Notre Dame are the winningest programs in college football, ranking first and second all-time in both winning percentage and total wins, any meeting between the two has special significance. No one who was in attendance will ever forget Desmond Howard's diving touchdown catch that secured the Wolverines' win over the Irish in 1991. A "phantom touchdown" helped Notre Dame to a 25–23 win in the 2002 meeting, but Michigan holds a 17–12–1 edge in the series and has taken three of the last five contests.

MINNESOTA

Michigan and Minnesota play every year for the Little Brown Jug. In 1903, Michigan coach Fielding H. Yost had misgivings about the purity of his team's water supply for its visit to Minneapolis to play the Golden Gophers. He dispatched a team manager to find a vessel of their own to hold the team's water during the game. A thirty-cent, five-gallon jug was purchased from a store in Minneapolis and served Yost's purpose. Michigan was riding a 28-game winning streak and had beaten the Golden Gophers in their last four meetings, but that 1903 game was a brawl and ended in a 6–6 tie. The jug had been inadvertently left behind in Minneapolis, and when Yost requested its return, he was told he would have to win it back. The two teams did not meet again until 1909, and Yost's Wolverines did indeed win it back, 15–6. Michigan has prevailed in 47 of the last 58 meetings with Minnesota, 31 of the last 33, has not lost to the Gophers since 1986 and now holds a 65–23–3 bulge in the series.

MICHIGAN HAS PREVAILED IN 47 OF THE LAST 58 MEETINGS WITH MINNESOTA, 31 OF THE LAST 33, HAS NOT LOST TO THE GOPHERS SINCE 1986 AND NOW HOLDS A 65-23-3 BULGE IN THE SERIES.

MICHIGAN STATE

The Wolverines ran roughshod over Michigan State in 2002 in a 49–3 triumph to bring their lead in the cross-state rivalry to 62–28–5. A four-foot-tall wooden statue — the Paul Bunyan Trophy — is awarded annually to the winner of the contest. The trophy was donated by then-Michigan Governor G. Mennen Williams in 1953, the year Michigan State joined the Big Ten Conference. Since then, Michigan has won 29 of the 50 meetings between the two teams. The Wolverines have emerged victorious from five of the last seven matchups with the Spartans.

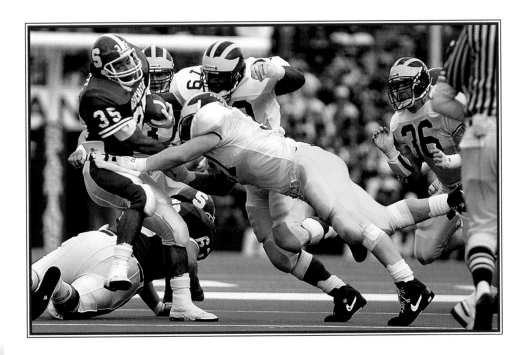

GREAT TEAMS

1 9 0 1 - 1 9 0 5 (5 5 — 1 — 1)

Fielding H. "Hurry Up" Yost coached Michigan through the first quarter of the twentieth century. His first five teams — his immortal "Point-a-Minute" teams — scored 2,821 points to their opponents' 42. From 1901 through 1904, Michigan did not lose a game and won the national title all four years. Yost chose his 1902 "Heston Backfield" as the best of his coaching tenure. With Willie Heston at left half, Albert Herrnstein at right half, Everett Sweeley at end and Harrison Weeks at quarterback, the '02 Wolverines outscored their opponents 644—12 on the way to an 11—0 record. The previous year, Yost's first at the helm in Ann Arbor, Michigan finished 11—0 with a 550—0 total score. On New Year's Day, 1902, Yost took his team out to California to play in the inaugural Tournament of Roses game (now called the Rose Bowl) and beat his old employer, Stanford, 49—0. The game was so one-sided that 14 years passed before there was another one, replaced in the interim by events such as ostrich races.

1 9 2 3 (8 — 0)

Michigan captured the sixth national title of the Yost era in 1923, posting a perfect 8—0 mark for the season. Halfback Harry Kipke and center Jack Blott, both All-Americans, would go on to coach Michigan to championships in later years — Kipke as head coach, Blott as line coach. The 1923 Wolverines outscored the opposition 150—12 and pitched five shutouts.

1933 (7 – 0 – 1)

Coach Harry Kipke brought a national title to his alma mater in 1933 behind All-America linemen in center Charles Bernard, whom pro coaches called the greatest college player in the country that year, and tackle Frances "Whitey" Wistert. Quarterback Stanley Fay served as team captain. Only a tie with Minnesota, who would go on to win the national championship the next year, marred an otherwise perfect record. The 1933 Wolverine defense never allowed more than six points all year and held five of eight opponents scoreless.

YOST'S FIRST FIVE TEAMS – HIS IMMORTAL "POINT-A-MINUTE" TEAMS – SCORED 2,821 POINTS TO THEIR OPPONENTS' 42. FROM 1901 THROUGH 1904, MICHIGAN DID NOT LOSE A GAME AND WON THE NATIONAL TITLE ALL FOUR YEARS.

1940 (7 – 1)

The 1940 Wolverines finished third in the national rankings, their only blemish being a 7–6 loss to Minnesota, who went on to win the national championship that year. This was the squad that produced the first of Michigan's Heisman Trophy winners — halfback Tom Harmon. End Edward Frutig joined Harmon on that year's All-America team. Only three opponents managed to score at all on that 1940 Michigan team, captained by quarterback Forest Evashevski.

1 9 4 7 (1 0 − 0)

Few if any teams ever played offense with the precision and verve of Fritz Crisler's "Mad Magicians" of 1947. Their execution of the buck-lateral and spinner cycle out of the single-wing formation left opponents embarrassed and frustrated, often tackling two or three Michigan backs, neither of whom had the ball. Having two All-America halfbacks — Bob Chappuis, the Heisman Trophy runner-up, and Chalmers "Bump" Elliott — didn't hurt. Led by tackle Alvin Wistert, end Len Ford and linebackers Dan Dworsky and Rick Kempthorn, the '47 Michigan defense pitched five shutouts and gave up a total of 53 points all year. Gene Derricotte was the nation's premier punt returner. The Associated Press held a special post-bowl poll — a first — after Michigan's 49–0 throttling of USC in the Rose Bowl and replaced Notre Dame with Michigan at the top spot.

1 9 4 8 (9 - 0)

Crisler retired from coaching and left the team to Bennie Oosterbaan in 1948. With All-Americans in quarterback Pete Elliott, end Dick Rifenburg and tackle Alvin Wistert, the Wolverines extended their winning streak to 23 games, dating back to the middle of the 1946 season. Defensively there were five more shutouts and 44 total points surrendered. The Big Nine's no-repeat rule precluded a post-season trip, but Michigan repeated as national champion. Oosterbaan's national title in 1948 was the last by a first-year major-college head coach for 53 years.

1 9 6 4 (9 − 1)

Bump Elliott, one of the famous Mad Magicians of 1947, was now head coach at his alma mater. Tall, talented Bob Timberlake was an All-America quarterback. On October 17 against Purdue, Timberlake flew through the Boilermaker defense for a

54-yard touchdown run, cutting a 21–14 deficit to 21–20 with less than five minutes remaining. But Timberlake, the Big Ten's MVP that season, was stopped one foot short on the two-point try, leading to the only setback in an otherwise perfect season. With a 34–7 rout of Oregon State in the Rose Bowl, the 1964 Wolverines finished 9–1 and ranked No. 4 in both polls — one foot short of a national championship.

1970 – 74 (50 – 4 – 1)

Bo Schembechler's Michigan teams of the early seventies flirted with perfection, winning 50 of 55 games over five seasons. The star-studded units featured All-Americans in halfback Billy Taylor; offensive linemen Dan Dierdorf, Reggie McKenzie and Paul Seymour; defensive linemen David Gallagher and Henry Hill; linebackers Marty Huff and Mike Taylor; and defensive backs Thom Darden, Randy Logan and Dave Brown. The 1971 club took an 11–0 record to the Rose Bowl only to drop a one-point decision to Stanford.

1976 (10 – 2)

Michigan spent most of the 1976 season as the No. 1 team in the nation. The Wolverines were 8–0 on November 6, when a 16–14 loss at Purdue dropped them from the top spot. Rob Lytle amassed 1,469 rushing yards at 6.6 per carry on his way to Big Ten MVP honors that fall. Rick Leach was in his sophomore year and etching his name in the school's quarterback lore. All-America linebacker Calvin O'Neal broke his own school record with 153 tackles after posting 151 the previous season. A 51–0 romp over Stanford in Game 2 and a 22–0 blanking of Ohio State punctuated the season, with the Wolverines finishing third in both polls.

1 9 9 7 (1 2 — 0)

Michigan's first national championship in half a century came in 1997. Cornerback Charles Woodson became the first primarily defensive player ever to win the Heisman Trophy. He intercepted eight passes for the Wolverines and also lent his electrifying skills to the offensive side of the ball and the punt return unit. Brian Griese piloted a solid offense with such weapons as running back Chris Howard and receiver Tai Streets. Tight end Jerame Tuman and defensive end Glen Steele were All-Americans. The Wolverines cemented their title with a 20–14 win over Ohio State to conclude the regular season and a 21–16 Rose Bowl triumph over Washington State.

GREAT PLAYERS

NEIL SNOW (END–FULLBACK, 1898–1901)

Neil Snow played both fullback and end at Michigan. He was an All-American and captain of Fielding H. Yost's 1901 team as a senior. He capped off his playing career by scoring five touchdowns in the Wolverines' 49–0 rout of Stanford in the inaugural Tournament of Roses game, known today as the Rose Bowl.

WILLIE HESTON (HALFBACK, 1901–04)

Willie Heston was the spearhead of Yost's Point-a-Minute juggernauts. During Heston's playing career, the Wolverines won four national titles. In his time, no other ball-carrier could rival him. All four members of what Yost referred to as his "Heston Backfield" were explosive open-field runners, but Heston was unstoppable. The left halfback on Michigan teams that scored 2,326 points to their opponents' 40 and never lost a game over four years, Heston scored 72 touchdowns.

ADOLPH "GERMANY" SCHULZ (CENTER, 1904–08)

Germany Schulz was the center on Grantland Rice's all-time team. According to Rice: "There have been great centers through every year of American football, but the greatest center I ever saw was Germany Schulz . . . one of the fastest big men on any field." Schulz dominated games on both sides on the line of scrimmage, backing up the line on defense. He was a 1907 All-American and a member of the AP All-Time Team picked in 1951.

ALBERT BENBROOK (GUARD, 1908–10)

Albert Benbrook was the first of the great pulling guards. At 240 pounds — a giant for his day — Benbrook could outrun most backs. He was a two-time All-American of whom Walter Camp remarked, "He leads his mates across the line with his quick, ripping charge that simply smothers the opposition."

HARRY KIPKE (HALFBACK, 1920–23)

Harry Kipke earned three letters at Michigan in football, basketball and baseball. On the gridiron he was an All-America halfback in 1922. Kipke excelled as a ball carrier, passer, blocker and kicker, and he was a terrific defensive player. He was also the best punter in the nation during the early twenties. He was captain of the 8–0 national champion Wolverines as a senior in 1923, and he later returned to Ann Arbor as head coach of his alma mater from 1929–1937.

BENNY FRIEDMAN
(QUARTERBACK, 1923–26)

Friedman, a charter member of the College Football Hall of Fame, was the greatest passer of his day. According to his coach, Fielding Yost, "In Benny Friedman, I have one of the greatest passers and smartest quarterbacks in history. He never makes a mistake." George Little, a Yost assistant, left to become head coach at Wisconsin before Friedman's senior year. "I should have waited until Benny graduated," Little said. "In my first year as head coach at Madison, we lost only one game — to Michigan, 21–0. And Benny figured in all of the touchdowns. He was unstoppable." Friedman was a two-year All-American, in 1925 and '26.

BENNIE OOSTERBAAN (END, 1924–27)

The most interesting fact about Oosterbaan is that in 1948 he became the only man to win a national championship in his first year as a head coach, and he held that distinction for 53 years, until 2001. As a player, Oosterbaan was the finest pass receiver of his time. He was a three-time All-American, in 1925, '26 and '27 and was chosen on the All-Time All-America team in 1951. The Friedman-to-Oosterbaan connection was one of the most feared passing combos in history, and on defense, Oosterbaan consistently frustrated opposing ball carriers trying his end, including Red Grange.

TOM HARMON (HALFBACK, 1938–40)

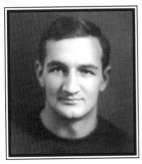

Tom Harmon teamed with quarterback Forest Evashevski to lift the Wolverines out of the football doldrums in the years immediately preceding World War II. Harmon led the nation in scoring in 1939 and 1940, finished second in Heisman balloting in 1939 and won the Heisman Trophy in 1940. Over his three seasons in Ann Arbor, Harmon ran for 2,134 yards and 33 touchdowns and threw 16 touchdown passes. In his last game for the Maize and Blue — the 1940 Ohio State showdown —"Old 98" rushed for 139 yards and two touchdowns, completed 11 of 12 passes for 151 yards and two more touchdowns, intercepted three passes, running one back for a score, and averaged 50 yards per punt, in a 40–0 Wolverine win.

BOB CHAPPUIS (HALFBACK, 1942, 1946–47)

Bob Chappuis had his football career interrupted by World War II — an aerial gunner, he was shot down on a mission over Italy and later escaped captivity — and picked up right where he left off in 1946. A true triple-threat halfback, Chappuis was an All-American and Heisman Trophy runner-up in 1947 for coach Fritz Crisler's national champs. On New Year's Day 1948, Chappuis set two Rose Bowl records, for total offense and pass completions.

CHALMERS "BUMP" ELLIOTT (HALFBACK, 1946–47)

Chappuis wasn't the only All-America halfback for the 1947 Wolverines; Bump Elliott joined him in the honor. Crisler called Elliott the greatest right halfback he ever saw. He led the Big Nine in scoring as a senior with 54 points and was named the conference's MVP. He later returned to Michigan as head coach and led the Maize and Blue to the Big Ten and Rose Bowl titles in 1964.

RON KRAMER (END, 1953–56)

Ron Kramer earned nine letters at Michigan — three each in football, basketball and track. He led both the football team and the basketball team in scoring for two seasons. He was a standout on both sides of the ball and was particularly dangerous as a receiver. A 230-pound high-jumper in track, Kramer was a consensus All-America end for two years (1955 and '56). His football jersey number 87 was retired following his senior year, and he went on to an all-pro career with Vince Lombardi's Green Bay Packers in the early sixties.

BOB TIMBERLAKE (QUARTERBACK, 1962–64)

Tall, talented Bob Timberlake quarterbacked Michigan to the Big Ten and Rose Bowl titles in 1964. He was MVP of the Big Ten, consensus All-America and finished fourth in that year's Heisman voting.

BILL YEARBY (TACKLE, 1963–65)

Bill Yearby was one of the best defensive tackles in the nation in the mid sixties. He was blessed with both strength and great speed and was best known for his prowess in pursuit.

RON JOHNSON (HALFBACK, 1966–68)

During his three-year college career, Ron Johnson virtually rewrote the Michigan rushing record book. Among the school standards he set were those for single-season and career rushing yardage. He also left Ann Arbor with eight new Big Ten marks. Johnson was two-time team MVP and was an All-American and Big Ten MVP in 1968.

DAN DIERDORF (OFFENSIVE TACKLE, 1968–70)

Dan Dierdorf was a two-time All-Big Ten and 1970 All-America offensive tackle. After his college career, Dierdorf went on to an all-pro career with the St. Louis Cardinals and was twice named the NFL's top offensive lineman.

REGGIE MCKENZIE (OFFENSIVE GUARD, 1969–71)

A consensus All-American as a senior in 1971, Reggie McKenzie is recognized as one of the game's greatest pulling guards. McKenzie helped clear the way for two Big Ten titles and Rose Bowl appearances.

BILLY TAYLOR (HALFBACK, 1969–71)

Billy Taylor was MVP of the 1971 Big Ten champion Wolverine team that finished with a perfect 11–0 regular season before dropping the Rose Bowl by one point. He exited Michigan after his senior year with the school's career rushing record of 3,072 yards and was second only to Tom Harmon with 32 rushing touchdowns. Taylor was a three-time All-Big Ten selection and a 1971 All-American.

THOM DARDEN (DEFENSIVE BACK, 1969–71)

One of the best punt returners in Michigan history, Darden was a three-year regular in the defensive backfield, starting and excelling at all four positions. Of his 11 career interceptions, Darden notched touchdown returns of 92 and 60 yards.

DAVE BROWN (DEFENSIVE HALFBACK, 1972–74)

Brown intercepted nine passes in his college career and also had an 88-yard punt return to his credit. He was co-captain of Bo Schembechler's 1974 Big Ten champs, was a three-time all-conference pick and a two-year All-American, in 1973 and '74.

ROB LYTLE (RUNNING BACK, 1974–76)

A consensus All-American, the Big Ten's MVP and third-highest Heisman vote-getter in 1976, Rob Lytle left Michigan after his senior year in possession of the school records for rushing in a single season and career. In the 1976 Michigan State game, Lytle averaged 18 yards on 10 carries.

MARK DONAHUE (OFFENSIVE GUARD, 1975–77)

Donahue was a two-time consensus All-American — the thirteenth Michigan player to be so honored twice — and was one of the greatest pulling guards in school history.

RICK LEACH (QUARTERBACK, 1975–78)

Rick Leach, a gunslinging southpaw, broke all of Michigan's career passing, total offense and touchdown records that had stood before him. He was All-Big Ten for three years, and in his senior year—1978—he was an All-American, finished third in the Heisman voting and was named the Big Ten's Most Valuable Player.

ANTHONY CARTER (WIDE RECEIVER, 1979–82)

The Big Ten hadn't had a three-time All-American in 36 years, until Michigan wide receiver Anthony Carter pulled it off in 1980, '81 and '82. He was the first 3,000-yard pass receiver in conference history. During his time in Ann Arbor, Carter caught 161 passes for 3,076 yards and 37 touchdowns and scored 40 touchdowns in all. He set an NCAA all-purpose running mark with a 17.4-yard average. In his senior year, he finished fourth in the Heisman Trophy balloting.

JOHN ELLIOTT (OFFENSIVE TACKLE, 1984–87)

John "Jumbo" Elliott was a four-year starting offensive tackle and a two-year consensus All-American. He was a first-round pick in the 1988 NFL Draft and enjoyed a 14-year pro career with the New York Giants and Jets.

JIM HARBAUGH (QUARTERBACK, 1983–1986)

Quarterback Jim Harbaugh completely rewrote Michigan's passing record book. He led the nation in pass efficiency in 1985, and his 2,729 passing yards in 1986 is a school record that still stands. He quarterbacked the Wolverines to a Fiesta Bowl victory following the 1985 season and the Big Ten title in 1986. As a senior in '86, Harbaugh was chosen Big Ten Player of the Year and finished third in the Heisman voting.

MARK MESSNER (DEFENSIVE TACKLE, 1985–88)

Messner was a two-year All-America defensive tackle who graduated from Michigan with more tackles for loss (70) for more lost yardage (376) than anyone who had gone before him. Messner started all 49 games of his college career and led the Wolverines in sacks three straight years.

TRIPP WELBORNE (SAFETY, 1987–90)

After converting from wide receiver to defensive back following his freshman year, Sullivan A. "Tripp" Welborne notched nine career interceptions and 238 tackles. He was a record-breaking punt returner and a two-year All-American, in 1989 and 1990.

DESMOND HOWARD (WIDE RECEIVER, 1989–91)

In 1991, Desmond Howard became Michigan's second Heisman Trophy winner, joining Tom Harmon on the list. Howard was the most electrifying player in college football in his day. He was the first receiver ever to lead the Big Ten in scoring, and he set a handful of NCAA records in the process. His received more first-place Heisman votes than anyone else before him, and also captured the Walter Camp and Maxwell Awards as a senior.

GREG SKREPENAK (OFFENSIVE TACKLE, 1988–91)

Greg Skrepenak was a four-year starting offensive tackle for the Wolverines, and his 48 consecutive starts were at the time a school record. He was a two-year All-American and a finalist for both the Outland Trophy and Lombardi Award.

CHARLES WOODSON (CORNERBACK, RECEIVER, 1995–97)

In 1997, Michigan's Charles Woodson became the first primarily defensive player ever to win the Heisman Trophy. He took over as a starter in the second game of his freshman year and never relinquished the job. He was named Big Ten Player of the Year twice. As a senior in 1997, Woodson picked off eight enemy aerials and was voted MVP of Michigan's national champions.

STEVE HUTCHINSON (GUARD, 1997–2000)

Steve Hutchinson was a four-year starter at guard and a two-time team captain. He was first-team All-Big Ten four straight years, did not allow a sack in either of his final two seasons and was a two-year All-American.

THE WISTERTS

Francis, Albert and Alvin Wistert are the only threesome of brothers to all be named first-team All-America. All three were tackles, and all three wore the number 11 jersey, which has since been retired in their honor. Francis "Whitey" Wistert was an All-American as a senior in 1933 when coach Harry Kipke's Wolverines won the national championship. In Francis' four years, Michigan posted a record of 31–1–3. Albert, also known as the "Ox," was an All-American and team MVP in 1942, then went on to an all-pro career with the Philadelphia Eagles. Alvin "Moose" Wistert was the oldest Michigan football player ever, thanks in large part to a four-year stint in the Marines during World War II before enrolling in 1946. Alvin was a two-time All-American, in 1948 and '49.

MICHIGAN IN THE COLLEGE FOOTBALL HALL OF FAME

COACHES

NAME	YEARS	INDUCTED
Fritz Crisler	1937–1947	1954
George Little	1922–1924	1955
Glenn E. "Bo" Schembechler	1969–1989	1993
Elton "Tad" Wieman	1921–1928	1956
Fielding Yost	1901–1924, 1926	1951

PLAYERS

NAME	POSITION	YEARS	INDUCTED
Albert Benbrook	Guard	1908–1910	1971
Anthony Carter	Wide Receiver	1979–1982	2001
Bob Chappuis	Halfback	1942, 1946–47	1988
Dan Dierdorf	Tackle	1968–1970	2000
Chalmers "Bump" Elliott	Halfback	1946–1947	1989

NAME	POSITION	YEARS	INDUCTED
Pete Elliott	Quarterback	1945–1948	1994
Bennie Friedman	Quarterback	1924–1926	1951
Tom Harmon	Halfback	1938–1940	1954
Willie Heston	Halfback	1901–1904	1954
Elroy Hirsch	Halfback	1943	1974
Ron Johnson	Halfback	1966–1968	1992
Harry Kipke	Halfback	1921–1923	1958
Ron Kramer	End	1954–1956	1978
John Maulbetsch	Halfback	1914–1916	1973
Reggie McKenzie	Guard	1969–1971	2002
Harry Newman	Quarterback	1930–1932	1975
Bennie Oosterbaan	End	1924–1927	1954
Merv Pregulman	Guard/Tackle	1941–1943	1982
Adolph "Germany" Schulz	Center	1904–1908	1951
Neil Snow	End/Fullback	1898–1901	1960
Ernie Vick	Center	1917–1921	1983
Bob Westfall	Fullback	1938–1941	1987
Albert Wistert	Tackle	1938–1942	1968
Alvin Wistert	Tackle	1946–1949	1981
Francis Wistert	Tackle	1930–1933	1967

TALKING MICHIGAN FOOTBALL

JON JANSEN, MICHIGAN OFFENSIVE TACKLE, AFTER THE WOLVERINES' 21–16 WIN OVER WASHINGTON STATE IN THE ROSE BOWL GAVE MICHIGAN THE 1997 NATIONAL CHAMPIONSHIP:

"It was a great experience. It's just a great feeling. Nothing that happens now will take away from what we did as a team. We played the toughest schedule and went 12–0. We feel we're the best team in the country right now."

"I think every guy who has played at Michigan takes great pride in this."

COACH LLOYD CARR, ON THE 1997 CHAMPIONSHIP

SAM SWORD, LINEBACKER, PRIOR TO THE 1997 PENN STATE GAME, WON BY MICHIGAN 34–8 IN HAPPY VALLEY:

"These are the types of games when championships are won. We've got to go in there and take their stadium over." Mission accomplished.

BO SCHEMBECHLER, U-M LEGEND, ON THE 1997 CHAMPIONSHIP DEFENSE:

"This is as good a defense as I've seen since I've been here. And it may be the best." And he would know.

"We didn't use a single substitute. After the game, we were enjoying ourselves in the hotel lobby when (Coach Fielding) Yost suddenly became aware that our three substitutes were missing. He asked Dan McGugin, our left guard (and longtime Vanderbilt coach) and me to look them up. We found them in back turning a garden hose on each other and rolling in the dirt — in full uniform. They told us they were ashamed to go home and have it known they hadn't gotten in the game."

MICHIGAN IMMORTAL WILLIE HESTON, ON THE FIRST ROSE BOWL GAME,
WON BY MICHIGAN 49–0 OVER STANFORD.

"Forty-six years and them bums ain't improved a lick."

AN ONLOOKER OBSERVING THAT MICHIGAN WON ITS FIRST TWO ROSE BOWL APPEARANCES,
IN 1902 AND 1948, BY IDENTICAL 49–0 SCORES.

"Michigan showed such a superlative poise and versatility in every department, such a wealth of offensive weapons and the talent to use them that it seemed a sacrilege to mention any other college team in the same breath."

LEGENDARY SPORTSWRITER RED SMITH ON MICHIGAN'S 1947 TEAM, WHICH WAS CROWNED
NATIONAL CHAMPION IN A SPECIAL VOTE TAKEN AFTER THE BOWL GAMES.

(Michigan trounced Southern Cal 49–0 in the Rose Bowl, while regular-season national champion Notre Dame had beaten the Trojans 38–7.)

"HE WAS BETTER THAN RED GRANGE, THE 'GALLOPING GHOST.'

Tom could do more things. He ran, passed, punted, blocked, kicked off, and kicked extra points and field goals. He was a superb defensive player."

MICHIGAN COACH FRITZ CRISLER ON THE IMMORTAL TOM HARMON.

"Taylor's to the 20, down to the 15, down to the 10, the 5. Four, three, two, one. Touchdown Billy Taylor! Touchdown Billy Taylor! Billy Taylor scored a touchdown from 21 yards out! Old man Ufer's been broadcasting for 27 years, and I have never seen anything like this! Oh. Oh my eyes! I'm an old man. I've got maize and blue spots in front of me right now."

BOB UFER'S LEGENDARY CALL OF THE WINNING TOUCHDOWN IN MICHIGAN'S 10–7 WIN OVER OHIO STATE IN 1971.

"Bo is to Michigan what macaroni is to cheese.

He means more to the state than any particular individual, and it's obvious from walking through campus that his leaving has had a tremendous impact at a time when students should be studying for finals."

MICHIGAN STUDENT ADAM SCHRAGER, ON THE OCCASION OF BO SCHEMBECHLER'S RETIREMENT.

"He's a decent guy. He's honest. He worked hard and he knew a little football."

SCHEMBECHLER, ON HOW HE'D LIKE TO BE REMEMBERED.

BOWL GAME TRADITION

1902 Rose Bowl	Michigan 49, Stanford 0
1948 Rose Bowl	Michigan 49, Southern California 0
1951 Rose Bowl	Michigan 14, California 6
1965 Rose Bowl	Michigan 34, Oregon State 7
1970 Rose Bowl	Southern California 10, Michigan 3
1972 Rose Bowl	Stanford 13, Michigan 12
1976 Orange Bowl	Oklahoma 14, Michigan 6
1977 Rose Bowl	Southern California 14, Michigan 6
1978 Rose Bowl	Washington 27, Michigan 20
1979 Rose Bowl	Southern California 17, Michigan 10
1979 Gator Bowl	North Carolina 17, Michigan 15
1981 Rose Bowl	Michigan 23, Washington 6
1981 Bluebonnet Bow	Michigan 33, UCLA 14
1983 Rose Bowl	UCLA 24, Michigan 14
1984 Sugar Bowl	Auburn 9, Michigan 7
1984 Holiday Bowl	BYU 24, Michigan 17
1986 Fiesta Bowl	Michigan 27, Nebraska 23
1987 Rose Bowl	Arizona State 22, Michigan 15
1988 Hall of Fame Bowl	Michigan 28, Alabama 24
1989 Rose Bowl	Michigan 22, Southern California 14
1990 Rose Bowl	Southern California 17, Michigan 10
1991 Gator Bowl	Michigan 35, Mississippi 3
1992 Rose Bowl	Washington 34, Michigan 14
1993 Rose Bowl	Michigan 38, Washington 31

1994 Hall of Fame Bowl	Michigan 42, NC State 7
1994 Holiday Bowl	Michigan 24, Colorado State 14
1995 Alamo Bowl	Texas A&M 22, Michigan 20
1997 Outback Bowl	Alabama 17, Michigan 14
1998 Rose Bowl	Michigan 21, Washington State 16
1999 Citrus Bowl	Michigan 45, Arkansas 31
2000 Orange Bowl	Michigan 35, Alabama 34
2001 Citrus Bowl	Michigan 31, Auburn 28
2002 Citrus Bowl	Tennessee 45, Michigan 17
2003 Outback Bowl	Michigan 38, Florida 30

1902 ROSE BOWL
MICHIGAN 49, STANFORD 0

The Tournament of Roses had been celebrated on New Year's Day in Pasadena for more than a decade with a parade and various sporting events before a football game was added to the festivities in 1902. Michigan, "The Champion of the West," was invited to play Stanford, the Pacific champion, in that first Tournament of Roses football game. The crowd of 8,000 on hand at Tournament Park witnessed Michigan run for 527 yards to Stanford's 67 in the 49–0 rout. Halfback Willie Heston picked up 170 of Michigan's yards, with fullback Neil Snow scoring five touchdowns. The game was called with over eight minutes left to go as Stanford captain Ralph Fisher was delegated to concede the victory to the visitors. Michigan coach Fielding Yost had been let go as Stanford coach after the previous season because of a rule calling for Pac-10 grads exclusively to coach Pac-10 teams. The outcome was so lopsided that the Tournament of Roses committee replaced the football game with chariot races, ostrich races and polo for the next 14 years before football was resumed in 1916.

1948 ROSE BOWL
MICHIGAN 49, SOUTHERN CALIFORNIA 0

Michigan's second bowl game, the 1948 Rose Bowl, ended like the first — in a 49–0 triumph. The victim this time was Southern California. Led by Heisman Trophy runner-up Bob Chappuis and Big Nine MVP Bump Elliott at the halfbacks, the Wolverines outgained the Trojans 491 yards to 133. Michigan scored in every quarter, took a 21–0 advantage into the locker room at halftime, and tacked on seven more points in the third quarter and 21 more in the fourth. Notre Dame was ranked No. 1 at the time and had beaten USC 38–7 to conclude the regular season, but the Associated Press held a special poll after the bowl games to oust Notre Dame from the top spot and replace the Irish with Michigan as 1947 National Champion.

1951 ROSE BOWL
MICHIGAN 14, CALIFORNIA 6

Michigan brought a 5–3–1 record to Pasadena to face fourth-ranked California in the 1951 Rose Bowl. Needless to say, the Golden Bears were favored to win. It was a tale of two halves. Cal outgained Michigan 192–65 and racked up a 10–2 edge in first downs in the first half, and took a 6–0 lead by intermission. In the second half, coach Bennie Oosterbaan's Wolverines picked up 226 total yards and 15 first downs to 52 yards and two first downs for California. And in the most important stat, fullback Don Dufek ran for two Michigan touchdowns in the fourth quarter for the 14–6 win.

1965 ROSE BOWL
MICHIGAN 34, OREGON STATE 7

Michigan finished the 1964 regular season with an 8–1 record, the Big Ten title and a fourth-place national ranking. Oregon State came into Pasadena 8–2 and ranked eighth nationally. After a scoreless first quarter, the Beavers drew first blood early in the second on a five-yard TD pass from Paul Brothers to Doug McDougall. Later in the second quarter, Wolverine tailback Mel Anthony scored on an 84-yard run, opening the floodgates. A 43-yard touchdown gallop by Carl Ward put Michigan up 12–7 at the half. Game MVP Anthony scored twice more in the third quarter and quarterback Bob Timberlake tacked on a 24-yard touchdown run down the sideline in the fourth, and Michigan found itself 34–7 victors and 4–0 all-time in the postseason.

1981 ROSE BOWL
MICHIGAN 23, WASHINGTON 6

Michigan lost Games 2 and 3 of 1980 by a combined total of five points, then rattled off eight straight wins, including three consecutive shutouts, and traveled to Pasadena on New Year's Day having not surrendered a touchdown over the last 18 quarters. After the Rose Bowl win over Pacific-10 champion Washington, the streak stood at 22 quarters. The Huskies managed just two field goals on the day. Wolverine tailback Butch Woolfolk ran for 182 yards, including a six-yard touchdown run that put Michigan up 7–6 at halftime. Quarterback John Wangler and wide receiver Anthony Carter connected on a third-quarter touchdown pass. Michigan kicker Ali Haji-Sheikh added a 25-yard field goal and Don Bracken set a Rose Bowl record with a 73-yard punt. The 1–2 start to the season ended in a nine-game winning streak and a No. 4 ranking in both polls.

1986 FIESTA BOWL
MICHIGAN 27, NEBRASKA 23

Michigan ended the 1985 regular season at 9–1–1 and boasted the nation's best scoring defense. Nebraska had won nine straight, sandwiched between losses in the opener and the finale. The two conference runners-up met in the Fiesta Bowl. A

42-yard field goal by Michigan's Pat Moons, set up by a 21-yard Jamie Morris run, was the extent of the scoring in the first quarter. Nebraska scored twice in the second quarter, on a short pass from McCathorn Clayton to Doug DuBose and a three-yard DuBose run, and the first half ended with the good guys trailing 14–3. But the Wolverines stormed back with 24 unanswered points in the third quarter, including a pair of short TD plunges by quarterback Jim Harbaugh, and held on for the win. Michigan forced six Cornhusker fumbles on the day, recovering three, and Dave Arnold blocked a punt to set up a short Moons field goal in the third quarter. With the win, Michigan finished the season ranked second nationally in both polls.

1988 HALL OF FAME BOWL
MICHIGAN 28, ALABAMA 24

With Bo Schembechler recuperating from heart surgery, offensive coordinator Gary Moeller assumed coaching duties for the 1988 Hall of Fame Bowl against Alabama. On the game's opening possession, the Crimson Tide marched to the

Michigan 34 and broke the ice with a 51-yard field goal. The Wolverines took control of the game in the second quarter with touchdown runs of 25 and 14 yards by Jamie Morris to take a 14–3 halftime lead. In the third quarter, Morris exploded for a 77-yard touchdown run, extending the margin to 21–3. But the Tide took the lead on 21 unanswered points. With a 16-yard pass from Jeff Dunn to Howard Cross and two Bobby Humphrey touchdown runs, Bama led 24–21 with less than five minutes to go. With the clock winding down and Michigan facing fourth and three, quarterback Demetrius Brown hit flanker John Kolesar on a 20-yard touchdown strike for the 28–24 win. Morris ran for a Hall of Fame Bowl record and Michigan bowl-game record 234 yards.

1989 ROSE BOWL
MICHIGAN 22, SOUTHERN CALIFORNIA 14

Bo Schembechler took his eleventh-ranked Wolverines out to Pasadena to face once-beaten, fifth-ranked USC, led by Heisman Trophy runner-up Rodney Peete at quarterback, in the 1989 Rose Bowl. Michigan picked up where it had left off at the end of the previous season's Hall of fame Bowl—with Demetrius Brown connecting with John Kolesar for 21 yards to set up a 49-yard Mike Gillette field goal. The first quarter ended 3–0 Michigan, but Peete scored twice on short runs in the second for a 14–3 Southern Cal lead at the half. That would close the book on the Trojans' scoring for the day. In the third, Brown scrambled 22 yards to the USC 6, then hit Chris Calloway on a six-yard scoring toss two plays later. A 23-yard Brown-to-Derrick Walker pass and a 61-yard Leroy Hoard run set up a pair of one-yard scoring plunges by Hoard in the fourth quarter. Linebacker John Milligan iced the victory with an interception of a Peete aerial with 50 seconds left. Hoard shredded the USC defense—the Pac-10's best that year—for 142 rushing yards on 19 carries. With the win, the Wolverines vaulted into fourth place in the final AP poll.

1991 GATOR BOWL

MICHIGAN 35, MISSISSIPPI 3

Gary Moeller's first Michigan team put the finishing touches on a 9–3 campaign with a 35–3 dismantling of Southeastern Conference runner-up Ole Miss in the Gator Bowl. The Rebels scored once, on a Gator Bowl record 51-yard field goal by Brian Lee in the second quarter. The Wolverines had opened the scoring in the first quarter on a 63-yard touchdown pass from Elvis Grbac to Desmond Howard, and finished the rout with a 33-yard Grbac-to-Derrick Alexander connection in the fourth. Howard found himself on the receiving end of two Grbac scoring tosses — the second came early in the third quarter and covered 50 yards. Two Wolverine running backs—Jon Vaughn and Ricky Powers—exceeded the 100-yard rushing mark. Michigan amassed 715 yards of total offense, and for their efforts offensive linemen Dean Dingman, Tom Dohring, Greg Skrepenak, Matt Elliott and Steve Everitt were named the game's Most Valuable Players.

1998 ROSE BOWL

MICHIGAN 21, WASHINGTON STATE 16

Michigan added emphasis to its most recent national title with a 21–16 Rose Bowl victory over Pac-10 champion Washington State. A 15-yard scoring pass from Ryan Leaf to Kevin McKenzie put the Cougars on top 7–0 to end the first quarter. In the second, Michigan QB Brian Griese and wide receiver Tai Streets connected on the first of two long touchdown passes, from 53 yards out, to knot the score at 7–7 entering intermission. In the third period, Leaf engineered a 99-yard drive that culminated in a 14-yard reverse by wide receiver Michael Tims to reclaim the lead for the Cougars. Michigan's James Hall blocked the PAT attempt and the score remained 13–7. Then came Griese-to-Streets II — a 58-yard scoring bomb that put the Wolverines up to stay, 14–13. In the fourth quarter, Griese found tight end Jerame Tuman from 23 yards out to extend the lead to 21–13. Washington State added a field goal to pull within striking distance at 21–16, but Michigan held the ball for the next seven minutes, converting four third downs in the process, and time ran out on the Cougars. Griese received game MVP honors on the strength of an 18-for-30, 251-yard, three-touchdown passing performance. And the 12–0 Wolverines were national champions for the 11th time.

1999 CITRUS BOWL
MICHIGAN 45, ARKANSAS 31

Michigan emerged victorious from its top-20 matchup with Arkansas in the 1999 Citrus Bowl. The Wolverines scored first on a 43-yard first-quarter field goal by Jay Feeley, but found itself trailing 31–24 with 5:49 left to play. Coach Lloyd Carr's troops responded with 21 unanswered points in just 4:02 of playing time for the 45–31 win. A 21-yard touchdown pass from Tom Brady to DiAllo Johnson put the Wolverines ahead to stay. Anthony Thomas, Michigan's all-time leading rusher, ran for 139 yards and three touchdowns on the day, and was awarded game MVP honors. Linebacker Sam Sword paced the Michigan defense with 11 tackles.

2000 ORANGE BOWL
MICHIGAN 35, ALABAMA 34

The Maize and Blue had to overcome 14-point deficits twice to score a 35–34 win over Alabama in the 2000 Orange Bowl, the first overtime game in Michigan history. Both teams entered the game with Top-10 national rankings. After a scoreless first quarter, the Crimson Tide took a 14–0 lead in the second on a pair of Shaun Alexander touchdown runs. The Wolverines answered with a 27-yard scoring pass from Tom Brady to David Terrell to close the gap to 14–7 at halftime, and a 57-yard Brady-to-Terrell strike in the third quarter knotted the score at 14. But the third-quarter fireworks had just started. Bama took another two-touchdown lead on a 50-yard Alexander run and a 62-yard Freddie Milons punt return, and Michigan pulled even with a 20-yard TD pass from Brady to Terrell and a three-yard Thomas touchdown run — all in the third quarter. A scoreless fourth period left the score tied 28–28 after regulation. Brady hit tight end Shawn Thompson on a 25-yard scoring strike on Michigan's first play in overtime, and Hayden Epstein made what turned out to be the game-winning extra point. After Andrew Zow connected with Antonio Carter from 21 yards out to pull within one, Bama's PAT kick failed. Final score: Michigan 35, Alabama 34.

2003 OUTBACK BOWL
MICHIGAN 38, FLORIDA 30

Michigan quarterback John Navarre completed 21 of 36 pass attempts for 319 yards, and Florida's Rex Grossman went 21-of-41 for 323 yards. But it was the Chris Perry show. Michigan's junior running back ripped Florida's defense for 193 yards — 85 rushing and 108 receiving — and scored four touchdowns in a 38–30 win over the Gators in the 2003 Outback Bowl. Perry's first score, a four-yard run, put the Maize and Blue up 7–0 in the first quarter. In the second, Earnest Graham gave the Gators a 13–7 lead on two touchdown runs, with a missed two-point try after the second. Michigan piled up the points, leading 21–16 at the half and 35–23 after three. Florida pulled within five on a three-yard scoring strike from Grossman to tight end Aaron Walker midway through the fourth period, then Michigan extended its lead to eight on a 33-yard Adam Finley field goal with 2:20 to play. Wolverine linebacker Victor Hobson sealed the 38–30 triumph with an interception of a wide receiver reverse pass with less than a minute to go and Florida driving.